ANNA PAVLOVA

THE DYING SWAN
(ballet dates from 1905, this costume from 1914)

1

DON QUIXOTE
(1908)

GISELLE
(1910; costume by Alexandre Benois)

THE DRAGONFLY
(ca. 1914)

BACCHANAL
(1910)

3

CHOPINIANA
(Les Sylphides; 1909; costume by Benois)

RUSSIAN DANCE
(ca. 1912; costume by Léon Bakst)

4

LES COQUETTERIES DE COLOMBINE
(1914)

GAVOTTE
(1914)

CALIFORNIAN POPPY
(ca. 1923)

LE PAVILLON D'ARMIDE
(1909; costume by Benois)

THE SNOWFLAKE
(1921)

MEXICAN DANCES
(1918)

SYRIAN DANCE
(ca. 1917)

AU BAL
(1914)

VASLAV NIJINSKY

LE PAVILLON D'ARMIDE
(1909; costume by Benois)

9

CHOPINIANA
(Les Sylphides; 1909; costume by Benois)

LE FESTIN
(1909; costume by Bakst)

LES ORIENTALES
(Kobold Dance; costume by Bakst)

LES ORIENTALES
(1909; costume by Bakst)

11

CARNAVAL
(1910; costume by Bakst)

SCHEHERAZADE
(1910; costume by Bakst)

GISELLE
(1910; the costume by Benois
that led to Nijinsky's break
with the Imperial Ballet in 1911)

THE SPECTRE OF THE ROSE
(1911; costume by Bakst)

13

PETROUCHKA
(1911; costume by Benois)

NARCISSUS
(1911; costume by Bakst)

THE BLUE GOD
(1912; costume by Bakst)

THE AFTERNOON OF A FAUN
(1912; costume by Bakst)

JEUX
(1913; costume by Paquin)

TILL EULENSPIEGEL
(1916; costume by Robert Edmond Jones)

16